911 Breakup Survival
How To Get Over A Breakup And Love Again, Like It's The First Time

Hadley Finch

ABOUT THE AUTHOR:

Hadley created the world's first guided love quest to help singles find great love in TribeOfSingles.com Love Matches- Love Vacations, and the TribeofCouples.com Love Toolkit which sustains passionate intimacy, romantic fun and undying devotion. She helps you cure a happiness deficiency during her coaching- luxury spa weekend at HappinessCoachingSPA.com

Hadley Finch is a love guide, who has experienced the intense pain of lost love and lost dreams after her long, happy marriage to a corporate superstar ended tragically. She shares her first-hand experiences and success secrets gained by working with the world's top experts to help you end heartbreak, rebound from tough challenges, revitalize your love life and relationships, pass love tests and move from being alone, or being bored to happiness and bliss.

Hadley is a graduate of Northwestern University, a former Emmy-nominated producer-writer in Chicago television, a certified teacher, and a proud mom of two children, both happily launched. She is excited to guide your journey from lost love to the fire of love, so you get all the love and happiness you deserve now.

Foreword by Raymond Aaron

You may be drawn to this book, because you are suffering from the pain of lost love and seeking a path out of pain. You get the urgent care you need now from America's Love Guide, Hadley Finch. She gives you the roadmap for the fastest, surest journey from lost love into the fire of love.

Hadley says we all deserve to burn in the fire of love by loving truly, deeply and passionately. When that dream of love dies through a breakup, divorce, or death of a beloved partner, she suggests that you make a conscious choice:

Choose to bury that dream of love in bitterness, fear and grief; or bring it back to life with a resilient, optimistic belief in great love.

Hadley admits how she'd struggled with this choice after her long, happy marriage ended tragically. When life as she knew it fell apart, she was tormented by fear and anger, which had made her heart feel like a pressure cooker ready to blow. Unable to sleep or eat well for months, she was afraid she might not survive the heartbreak of lost love.

Do you know that pain? Do you want to break free from the clutches of tormenting thoughts, feelings and actions that keep breaking your heart over and over again? Are you ready to end heartbreak and get all the love and happiness you deserve now?

You hold in your hands a revolutionary road map, which guides you around breakup minefields that destroy your health and happiness. Hadley had used this roadmap to heal her own trauma from lost love. And you will, too, as soon as you open your heart and mind to the truths you discover here:

Love survives the death of a relationship or a beloved partner. This means you cannot lose love. You learn to see its new form and let the healing power of love fuel your speedy recovery. You take the best shortcut on the journey from heartbreak to happiness simply by following this roadmap.

Does this sound too easy?

Whenever Hadley Finch hears this objection, she explains that she didn't invent this roadmap. She only pieced it together by exploring how you make life and universal laws work for you instead of against you, and use your greatest challenges as the gateway to your greatest triumphs.

She developed these love skills by working with the world's top experts and sharing proven success secrets and strategies in hundreds of articles, books, seminars and during interviews for her radio show, A Lasting Love.

Now she gives you exciting love skills to end heartbreak, break through hidden love blocks, bounce back from tough challenges, and build a great new life you love. So before you even think of putting down this guide, we encourage you to consider these options:

Will you spend years grieving and trying to shatter the illusion of lost love, like Hadley did?

Or will you use the love wisdom she's gained from ancient and modern teachers to speed up your brave journey from heartbreak to happiness?

You have at your fingertips the emergency relief and expert care you need to stop suffering, break free from the clutches of fear, anger or grief, and create a happy, new ending to your sad, old love story. You not only survive a breakup and thrive, but you also enjoy your guided quest to get all the love and happiness you deserve now.

911 Breakup Survival
Get Over A Breakup And Love Again, Like It's The First Time

Hadley Finch

Contents

Foreword by Raymond Aaron

Introduction: How America's Love Guide Survived A Devastating Breakup. And You Will, Too!

1. Beat Breakup Stress Before It Rewires Your Brain And Beats You
2. Can You Ever Recover Your Health After Divorce or Death Of A Spouse?
3. Grief Is Good, When You Take The Right Steps Through It
4. Want To Murder Your Ex? Use The BIG GUNS
5. Top 8 Tools To Manage Anger and Build A Better Life
6. Love Test - Will You Forgive, Or Let That Old Grudge Kill You?
7. Radical Forgiveness - Why You Can't Make Mistakes In Relationships
8. Turning Fear and Loneliness Into Love In 2 Steps
9. Write A Happy New Ending To Your Sad Old Love Story - Without Lying
10. Love Test - 8 Sure-Fire Signs You're Over Your Ex
11. Shocking Remedy Solves Love Problems Fast
12. Feeling Loved and Happy, No Matter Who Is Or Isn't Sleeping Beside You
13. Bouncing Back From Setbacks in 5 Steps
14. 4 Proven Steps to End The Toughest Addictions, Including Sex and Drugs
15. Creating The Future You Love Now
16. Love Test - What's Good About Floating In Hot Water For A Year?
17. Shot Down 7 Times, Bounce Back 8 - Plus 9 Guiding Principles For The Journey From Lost Love To The Fire Of Love
18. Love Test - What Kind Of Lover Is Happiest?
19. End Money Worries And Even Double Your Income Doing What You Love
20. 5 Ways To Love Again, As If It's The First Time
21. Your Gifts and Guides to Even Greater Love and Happiness

Introduction

How America's Love Guide Survived A Devastating Breakup. And You Will, Too!

I'm Hadley Finch, and I'm thankful you're here. You've found the urgent care you need to not only survive a breakup, but also thrive in your new life. You are about to discover the fastest, surest remedies to get over the pain of lost love and get back on the happiness track where you belong.

I've learned the hard way how to do this after my long, happy marriage ended tragically. I wrote this book to make sure you don't suffer needlessly, like I did.

I've learned how to heal heartbreak and fall in love with my new life by working with the world's top experts for over 10 years, by interviewing many of them and sharing great love tips during my radio show, A Lasting Love. Today, I'm known as America's Love Guide, because I help men and women find great love and create great relationships, using secrets of A Lasting Love.

Why should I be your love guide?

I know what you're going through. I am a love guide, who knows the intense pain of lost love and lost dreams. I hate to admit how low I sank while my marriage was breaking up. Yet I feel it's important to tell you my story, because it reveals how anyone can get hit by a tidal wave of pain, when life as you know it falls apart.

Let's turn back the clock to 1999. I'd been thinking, "Life is beautiful," while raising my wonderful pre-teen children and enjoying married life with my corporate superstar husband. Then BAM, my marriage was over.

When life slams you down, how do you get back up?

I'd struggled to bounce back, because I was tormented by destructive emotions and a desire for revenge against my husband, who'd left me to date a young woman. "A baby woman," I'd called her.

I was devastated, my heart feeling like a pressure cooker ready to blow. I was obsessed with one question: What was he thinking when he left me and our amazing family life?

I'd stayed awake nights for months, blaming him for our breakup, imagining his love scenes with her, and plotting ways to whack both of them. Poison. Car. Gun.

When I'd thought about signing up for shooting lessons, luckily something inside me said, "Whoa." I sought expert help and learned it was my mind, trying to take control of an uncontrollable situation. This was normal, unless I acted upon it.

Well, I did act on it. I put down my pistol in my mind, picked up my pen in my hand and vented my rage on the page. You've got to get anger out somehow, so I started writing about my anger at night when I couldn't sleep.

Normally a writer wants to take anger and intense emotions and turn them into a thing of beauty. What I was writing was so angry that people would have run from it, instead of read it.

Want to know when I changed that?

When my heart started hurting so much I was afraid I might die, I sought urgent care, asking, "Heart Attack? Or Heart Break?"

When tests showed it was heart break, not heart attack, I gave a long sigh of relief. Then the heart doctor gave me a wake up call, "You can die of a broken heart."

I'd researched this and learned that "broken heart syndrome" is a real condition resulting from intense emotional stress, which often stems from the death of a loved one, fear, extreme anger, or surprise. Such sudden and strong emotional stress can cause severe weakness of the heart muscle, which can result in low blood pressure, chest pain, shortness of breath, and even congestive heart failure.

To save my life, I had to take anger and stress off my heart fast. Doctor's orders.

I had to diffuse my desire to destroy my husband and his young mistress. You'll discover my emergency relief in the Chapter: Want to murder your ex? Use the BIG GUNS.

I had to use the power of anger productively. And you will, too, using tools in the Chapter: Top 8 Tools To Manage Anger and Build A Better Life

I had to make a shift in my thinking to stop being the victim and start being the creator of a great new life. You make this shift, by doing the exercises in two Chapters:

Love Test - Will You Forgive Or Let That Old Grudge Kill You?
Radical Forgiveness - Why You Can't Make Mistakes In Relationships

I had to give myself the urgent care that I'm sharing with you in each chapter, so you get through grief, recover your health, which often takes a beating in a breakup, solve your love problems fast, move from being lonely and afraid to happy and loved, and create the future you love right now.

As soon as I'd started using the new love skills you're about to discover, I'd noticed how my heart calmed down. How the words I'd been writing each night had started to rhyme, and the rhymes had formed verses of songs and the songs had formed an *album* that started with a breakup, moved through anger and grief phases, the reviving your dreams and dating again phases, and ending up in the Fire Of Love. 1/ Isn't that where we all want to be?

I help you get there. I show you how to let the pain of lost love open the doorway to the creative realm and a great new life. I show you shortcuts on your brave journey from heartbreak to happiness.

This book is the roadmap that guides you around breakup minefields, gives you new love skills to end heartbreak, start fresh and get all the love and happiness you deserve now.

What's your next step?

I encourage you to read this book from cover to cover, while marking the pages that speak to your heart and take weight off your shoulders.

After your first read-through, go back to read the pages that you've marked. Take the prescribed actions and use these new love skills to move from stress to joy.

After you take these action steps, then go back and re-read the book. Find out what speaks to you, now that you've beaten the toughest stress before it rewires your brain and beats you.

The pages you mark in your second read-through guide the next phase of your journey and give you new love skills to lift your spirits, improve your interactions and design the life and relationships you love.

1/ Listen to my album that starts with a breakup and ends in the Fire Of Love as my gift, simply by visiting www.TribeOfBlondesBonusMusic.com I share parts of my story throughout these chapters and in bonus gifts that show you how I got back on the happiness track and made my new single life even better than ever - and you will, too.

Are you curious how I'd made the same journey that you're beginning now?

I share parts of my story throughout these chapters and in bonus gifts that show you how I got back on the happiness track and made my new single life even better than ever -- and you will, too. 2/

Since we learn best by repetition, I suggest you keep re-reading this book, repeating the exercises and taking action on these new ideas until they become part of you. Remember a mind stretched by new ideas never shrinks back to its original dimension.

Are you ready to expand your mind, open your heart, get through grief, revive your dreams and fall in love again with yourself and your new life?

Let's get started.

2/ **Discover how I healed my heartbreak and started dating again after being married my whole adult life in your bonus gift novel, Tribe Of Blondes - Adventures of Breakup Survivors Seeking Love Online and Happiness In Relationships. Enjoy the first laptop novel that you read online, and it also includes songs,videos and an audiobook of my reading the unabridged novel to you. Gain instant access to your gift laptop novel when you visit** www.TribeOfBlondesGiftNovel.com

1.

Beat Breakup Stress Before It Rewires Your Brain and Beats You

Ever do crazy things since your breakup? You may be stuck in the "fight or flight" stress response.

Find out how persistent stress over lost love, lost dreams, lost security can rewire your brain, change your behavior and leave you vulnerable to serious illness. After you discover the health risks of breakup stress, you use the remedy that beats stress before it beats you.

What are the health risks of breakup stress?

Medical researchers have proven that persistent stress can raise blood pressure, harden arteries, harm your immune system and heighten your risks of diabetes, depression and Alzheimer's disease.

Persistent break up stress also can rewire the brain to promote a vicious cycle of habitual, destructive behavior. What are the symptoms? To find out, take this quiz:

* Have you experienced uncontrollable, repetitive thoughts or negative feelings about your lost love?
* Do you stay awake nights plotting ways to avenge a betrayal or broken vows?
* Do you obsessively call, email, or stalk your ex?
* Do you stop eating or overindulge in food, alcohol, drugs, or in any physical pleasure carried to a promiscuous excess?
* Do you ever feel you don't recognize yourself or your new habits, yet you can't seem to switch back to positive, goal-directed behaviors?

How'd you score?

If you answered YES to one or more questions, I'll give you incentive to change that:

There's new scientific evidence that these destructive behaviors become a habit faster when you're stressed.

"This is a great model for understanding why we end up in a rut, and then dig ourselves deeper and deeper into that rut," says Dr. Robert Sapolsky, a neurobiologist who studies stress at Stanford University Medical School.

"We are lousy at recognizing when our normal coping mechanisms aren't working," Dr. Sapolsky told the New York Times. "Our response is to do something five times more, instead of thinking, 'This isn't working, so maybe I should try something else.'"

How do you use this news?

These findings help you understand how an admirable trait like perseverance can be taken to extreme, uncontrollable repetition and become a perverse habit quickly, under chronic stress.

Breakup stress can be chronic, while you go through a divorce or custody battle, or while you grieve the death of a beloved partner.

What if you're stuck in rut of stress and uncontrollable negative habits?   How to you break out of it?

Fortunately, the brain is a very resilient and plastic organ. Dr. Bruce S. McEwen, head of the brain research lab at Rockefeller University, told the New York Times that his new findings prove that the brain's dendrites and synapses retract and reform. So reversible modeling can occur throughout our lifetime.

How did Dr. McEwen reach these findings?

His research team found that lab rats exposed to chronic stress remained hyperactive in a rut of negative behaviors--until they received the antidote.

The antidote was a four week vacation from stressors, while remaining in a supportive setting.

"Because the brain is resilient, it makes new synaptic connections in the decision-making regions of the pre-frontal cortex, while the dendrite vines of habit-prone sensori-motor striatum retreat," Dr. McEwen said.

How do these findings in lab rats help us?

We now realize that chronic stress changes your brain, and relaxation in a supportive environment changes it back.

How do you relax, when you're too stressed by your breakup?

If you can't take the recommended 4-week vacation to relax in a supportive environment, you can choose to make your health and well being a top priority. You become your own best friend and promise to take good care of yourself every day during your recovery and thereafter. How?

Use one or more of these relaxation tools to ease stress each day:

* Do some deep breathing, ideally during a walk in nature.
* Listen to guided relaxation tapes, instead of taking a caffeinated beverage break.
* Sign up for a series of therapeutic massages and biofeedback sessions, which release your energetic patterns of stress.
* Listen to guided visualization or hypnosis audios, which relieve stress, help you reach forgiveness and healing so you regain feelings of peace and confidence.
* Seek solace in your faith, your supportive friends and family.

This is the urgent care you give yourself every day to beat stress, protect your health, and get back on the happiness track where you belong.

What if your health has taken a beating, during your bout of lost love? Discover the remedy next…

2.

Can You Ever Recover Your Health After Divorce Or Death Of A Spouse?

University Of Chicago researchers have issued a health warning for married people who become single again, either through divorce or death of a spouse:

You may never fully recover from the emotional wounds and physical decline caused by marital loss, even if you remarry.

As we examine these medical findings, which were reported in the New York Times, you discover why newly-single adults must be vigilant about taking care of your health. And you learn how to relieve or prevent chronic health problems commonly experienced in divorced or widowed adults.

Why does the death of your marriage or your spouse cause chronic health problems?

"When your spouse is getting sick and about to die, or your marriage is getting bad and about to die, your stress levels go up," said Linda Waite, Ph.D., a sociology professor at the University of Chicago. Dr. Waite co-authored this study, which appears in the September 2009 issue of The Journal Of Health And Social Behavior.

"You're not sleeping well, your diet gets worse, you don't exercise, you don't see your friends. It's a whole package of awful events," said Dr. Waite. She and her research team studied the health effects of divorce, widowhood and remarriage in 8,652 people over time. Why?

"We recognize that the health benefits of marriage, already documented by a wealth of research studies, stem from several factors," Dr. Waite said. "Married couples are better off financially. They share employer health benefits and support each other in caring for their home, family and each other."

What happens when your marital health benefits are lost?

Dr. Waite's team found that divorced or widowed adults experienced 20 percent more chronic health problems, like heart disease, diabetes and cancer--compared with people who had been continuously married. Previously-married people in their 50's and beyond were more likely to have mobility problems, like difficulty climbing the stairs or walking a meaningful distance.

Does marrying again improve your health?

"Remarrying led to some improvement in health," Dr. Waite said. "Yet most married people, who became single, never fully recovered from their physical decline associated with marital loss."

This study does not prove that marital loss causes health problems. It may be that people who don't exercise, don't eat well and don't manage stress are more likely to get divorced. Yet Dr. Waite's researchers observed that these health problems were seen in divorced and widowed people alike, so the data strongly suggests a causal relationship.

How does marital loss cause health problems?

During times of high stress, we experience changes at the cellular level. How?

Dr. Waite's researchers at Ohio State University had focused on "telomeres," which insulate and protect the ends of our chromosomes. They found that people under stress of caring for Alzheimer patients had showed a pattern of shortened telomeres and less activity of a related enzyme. This could cause a 4-8 year shortening of their life span.

"The stress of divorce or widowhood might take a similar toll on our lifespan," Dr. Waite concluded.

Should spouses stay in a bad marriage for the sake of their health?

This is not recommended, since marital troubles can lower immune responses and lead to physical troubles. A series of experiments at Ohio State University revealed that wounds took longer to heal in people experiencing marital conflict and hostility, compared to people in supportive marriages.

In terms of health, is it better to have married and lost, than never to have married at all?

The research says, No. Middle-age people, who never married, have fewer chronic health problems than those who were divorced or widowed.

How does marrying again affect your health?

A second marriage appears to heal emotional wounds of marital loss. Remarried people in Dr. Waite's study showed only slightly more depressive symptoms than those continuously married.

How do you use these medical findings to improve your health?

These studies indicate that married people tend to be healthier than single people, unless you remain happily single throughout your whole adult life.

If marital loss can shorten your life and a supportive marriage with little animosity can prolong your life, then we have incentive to improve our marriages and improve the way we grieve the death of a marriage or a spouse.

Let's take the right steps through grief next...

3.
Grief Is Good, When You Take The Right Steps Through It

Grieving lost love can feel like a tidal wave of pain that hits often and without warning. Because grief can be so painful, some of us try to escape or deny the pain to get over it quickly.

Studies show that when people don't deal with the emotions of grief, the pain does not go away. It can be buried inside and rise up in hurtful ways.

Some people may be stuck in one phase of the grieving process, and they need help getting through it. One woman, who was stuck in grief, recently sent me an email asking this profound question, "How do I stop grieving a love I lost 25 years ago?"

Her lost love had been her first love. Though they each had married other people, she couldn't let go of the memory of their love story and the hope that they would reunite someday.

I helped her get unstuck and grow through grief with the information you're about to discover. To begin the healing process, let's address a common question that needs to be answered when you lose someone you love:

How long must you feel the anguish of grief, before you can heal it?

There is no normal timetable. We each grieve in our own way, in our own time.

People who grieve for decades may see this as proof of their undying love. Or they may not know how to move through each predictable phase of the grieving process.

People who move through grief, without getting stuck in one phase, may do so by holding in their heart the loving memory and legacy of their departed loved one. Or they find comfort in the belief that their loved one now is in a better place.

As mere mortals, each of us will face the death of a loved one and grieve in our own way. Do you know anyone who has been been taught how to say good-bye, or how to grieve and recover from the pain of lost love?

Few of us learn these love skills, before we need to use them. That's why you may need help to handle a tidal wave of grief, which can make you feel fragile, alone and unloved.

While in this vulnerable emotional state, you may not be able to embrace this truth:

Lost love is an illusion, because love never dies. It only changes form. When you learn to see and feel undying love and give thanks for it, you fill the devastating void in your heart with love.

This process is illustrated in a Sufi saying, "When the heart grieves over what it has lost, the spirit rejoices over what it has left."

One of life's greatest love tests is to let your spirit rejoice, even while you're knocked to your knees in grief. How do you lift your spirit and heal your grieving heart?

It helps to understand the grieving process and how to move through it. In the seminal 1969 book, On Death And Dying, author Elizabeth Kubler-Ross identified the predictable stages of grieving the death of someone you love. You go through the same trauma, while you grieve the death of a relationship.

As you grieve a loss, you may feel several emotions at the same time, in varying intensity, while you move through predictable stages of grief, which I've summarized from Elizabeth Kubler-Ross's On Death And Dying:

Shock
If a loving relationship ends suddenly, shock often is your first reaction. You may be numb and go through the motions of living, while feeling nothing. You may experience physical symptoms, such as confusion and loss of appetite.

Denial
After initial shock wears off, you may not want to accept the reality that your relationship is over. You may fantasize that your beloved will return, as if nothing has happened.

Anger
You may feel anger that you were betrayed and abandoned by your departed love. You may be angry at yourself for not doing enough to save your relationship. Your anger may be mild, or it may cause irrational thoughts and behavior.

Guilt
You may be haunted by angry words, selfish actions, or things you could have done to improve your relationship, if only you had known it was about to end.

Sadness
Once your anger has been exhausted, sadness may set in. You may feel alone and afraid. You may have little energy to get through your daily routine. You may try to stop yourself from crying, or you may experience crying episodes.

Acceptance

Time alone does not heal grief, unless you take certain actions. Acknowledging lost love and experiencing its pain frees you from the yearning to return to the past. Remembering the love and using your loving memories to create a new life without your loved one in it frees you to reach out for new relationships and new activities.

Growth

When you face the pain of grief, you may seek meaning in lost love and find a healthy path out of pain. As you learn your love lessons, you feel renewed energy to revive your dreams, begin new activities and create new relationships. This is your path of healthy personal growth.

Once you've grown through grief, how do your feelings change?

You may feel a new compassion for yourself, as a result of the pain you've experienced.

You may treat yourself with more kindness and become more sensitive to others, which frees you to develop richer relationships.

You may discover your new strength, emotional resources and independence, which delights you and frees you to enjoy your new life and find new love someday.

What if you can't reach the path of personal growth, because you're stuck in grief?

You can get unstuck from any stage of grief. You speed up your recovery, when you take as many of these actions as possible:

Feel Your Pain

Realize that grief is cyclical, so expect the emotions to come and go for weeks, months or even years, depending on the duration and depth of the loving relationship that you lost. Know that you have a natural need to express and release your sadness, even if it arises when you wish it would be long gone.

Talk About Your Sorrow

Seek comfort from friends, who will listen. Tell them you need to talk about your loss. If they change the subject, they may not know how to respond to your sadness. Turn to a pastor, life coach or grief counselor to help you get over the hurdles of grief.

Forgive Yourself

Forgive yourself for all the things you believe you should have said or done. Forgive yourself for the anger or embarrassment you may have felt while grieving lost love.

Eat Well and Exercise

Grief drains your energy. To revitalize, nourish your body with whole, unprocessed foods. Get out in nature and do some daily exercise - perhaps walking or riding bikes with friends, or in solitude. Exercise endorphins clear your mind and refresh your body.

Pamper Yourself

Take naps, read a good book, listen to your favorite music, soak in a tub, go to a ball game, rent a movie. Do something each day that is fun, distracting and comforting.

Take Daily Steps to Create a New Life

Seek a creative outlet to vent your grief. Write it out in a journal, sing or dance it out, laugh or cry it out by watching comedies or tear jerkers.

Releasing your grief revives your enthusiasm to look for interesting things to do. Some suggestions: Take courses, volunteer to coach a team or work for a pet cause, find a new job, meet new people in community, social, spiritual activities.

Should you start dating, while you are grieving lost love?

I encourage you to be cautious of dating, while grieving. It may be tempting to try to replace the person you've lost, before you heal your heartbreak. Doing so sets you up for even more heartbreak, because relationships built on rocky emotional ground often end badly. Why?

Once you grow through grief, you may find you have nothing in common with the person you chose, while feeling lost or needy. This person may prefer your needy state to the stronger person you become as you grow through grief. They may hold you back in unhealthy ways, until you feel the need to break up to protect your well being.

How do you avoid these painful scenarios?

You wait to date seriously until you discover the new you, who wants new things in a new relationship. As you grow through the grieving process, you fall in love again with yourself and your new life. Since like attracts like, your healthy self love attracts a like-hearted love match, whenever you're ready to find love again.

Now that you understand the predictable stages of the grieving process, can you guess where many people get stuck?

It's in the anger phase. If left unchecked, anger can harm your health and destroy your life or someone else's. To avoid that fate, use the urgent remedy you discover next...

4.
Want To Murder Your Ex? Use The BIG GUNS

The desire to avenge bad behavior is natural, unless it becomes an angry obsession. This can make your heart feel like a pressure cooker ready to blow. That's how I'd felt during my breakup, when I'd stayed awake at night for months, imagining my husband's love scenes with his young mistress and plotting ways to whack both of them.

As I told you earlier, I had to vent my anger to save my life. Heart Doctor's orders. How did I get urgent relief?

I had to use the BIG GUNS. That's my natural healer's term for the safest, most powerful remedies available. Before you try this at home, make sure there's no one around to hear you or see you. Then use the Big Guns by taking these steps:

* Find a photo of your ex (or the person, who's fueling your rage).
* Place that photo on a pillow, which you don't mind destroying.
* Grab a tennis racket with two hands and beat that photo.
* Shout, scream, vent your anger each time you blast the photo.
* Beat their image to shreds, and then dispose of the evidence.
* Place another photo on that pillow, if it survived, or a replacement.
* Repeat the process, blasting the BIG GUNS as often as needed to blow off steam and calm your heart.

Does this urgent remedy sound too drastic for you?

If so, you may not need it. Some anger-control experts suggest that taking these steps in your imagination may be equally effective. Visualize yourself kicking, beating and knocking your adversary off a cliff. If that mental exercise diffuses your rage, then use it.

Either way, this urgent remedy lowers your anger from a boiling point to a simmer. What are your next steps?

You disarm the causes of anger and avoid angry conflicts by using 8 new tools you discover next...

5.
Top 8 Tools to Manage Anger and Build An Even Better Life

You reverse the cause of anger and use it's power to improve your life, when you use the tools you're about to discover in highlights of my radio interview for A Lasting Love with Dr. Tony Fiore.

He's the nation's top anger control expert, with 35 years experience in giving anger management tools to individuals and law enforcement agencies.

Hadley: Why is it important to understand the cause of our anger?

Dr. Tony: Understanding the cause of anger helps you control it. People often express anger for three reasons:

When they don't get what they want
When they aren't being heard or validated
When they feel disconnected and want to be closer in a relationship.

Hadley: Is venting anger ever an effective communication tool?

Dr. Tony: The more anger you vent, the more you drive someone away. So venting anger doesn't help you get what you want, unless it's handled correctly by "Anger Venters." And also by "Anger Stuffers," who pretend they're not angry, when they really are angry deep inside.

Some people feel beyond anger, because their partner is lesser than them. Or they've given up trying to solve their anger problem. These are attitudes of contempt, which are the death blow to most relationships, and the greatest predictor of divorce.

Hadley: What if the breakup has happened, and now you're angry about it? How do you diffuse your anger and deal effectively with troubling issues?

Dr. Tony: I recommend using the top 8 tools to control anger and build a better life.

1. Reduce stress in your life and relationships.

When you're stressed, you react irrationally. Identify the issues that cause stress and either avoid or resolve them.

If caffeine revs up stress, you may have to give it up or switch to decaf. If anger boils up when your defenses are down under the influence of alcohol, then don't do alcohol and conflict resolution at the same time.

2. Develop empathy for the other person

See through their eyes, walk in their shoes, think their thoughts, so you understand what makes them angry. These insights help you resolve or avoid anger triggers.

3. Respond, instead of react

We react, when we do things automatically with certain triggers, like a knee-jerk reaction. Even though this doesn't bring us the results we want, we keep repeating the behavior.

We respond, when we choose behaviors that lead to positive outcomes. You can respond in new ways, which decrease the probability that you'll trigger an angry reaction from your partner.

4. Change your self talk

It's not as much about what someone did, as what we tell ourselves about what they did that triggers our anger. You can retrain your "self talk" about what you think of someone's behavior to change your emotional reaction to it.

Many times you over-react to things, because of your previous life experience or baggage. Once you're aware of your negative self talk, you replace it with positives, which lead to forward progress.

5. Use assertive communication

Let someone know where you stand on an issue, and then set your boundaries without offending them.

Speak calmly from your heart to their heart, so it isn't experienced as hostile criticism.

Understand that you can't change another person. You only can change your reaction to behavior or character traits that irritate you. When you start to change, you often pull different, improved behavior from your partner or other people in your life.

6. Adjust your expectations

Anger often is generated not by what happened, but because what happened is so different from what you expected. It's not that you expect less, so you won't be disappointed. It's just that you are realistic about what to expect in marriage or relationships, so you don't keep getting upset over things that may never change. Let your partner be who they are, and vice versa.

7. Forgive, but don't forget

You let go of resentment of hurtful things people did to you, instead of letting it fester for years. You don't forget what was done, and you won't allow it to happen again. Through forgiveness, you disconnect emotionally from it.

Forgiveness is a gift you give yourself, because it frees you from the pain of your past. If you don't give up the pain, it festers and will bring down the relationship.

8. Retreat and think things over

Take a "time out" to step back from an anger trigger, so you don't react in the usual ways. The amygdala is our reptilian brain, which is hard wired to destroy a threat. So you may need to consciously over-rule this reptilian brain and choose to behave in smarter ways.

Taking a time out is not like sweeping the issue under the rug; it's taking time to reflect and find out the best way to resolve an issue. In a calm moment, you go back to discuss and resolve the issue.

Hadley: What if you want to use these tools to manage anger, but your former partner or another volatile person refuses to use them?

Dr. Tony: If abusive, angry behavior doesn't stop, then it's best to protect yourself and separate from that relationship.

Again, when you start to change your own behaviors, you pull different behaviors from your partner. They will feel less defensive and act less angry. This is how you create positive changes in how people respond to you.

Hadley: Let's say you feel anger brewing inside you. What's the best way to avoid an angry blowup?

Dr. Tony: Your best choice is to see anger as a wake up call for positive action. When you begin to feel anger bubble up, take a deep breath and ask yourself four questions:

1. What can I learn from this irritation?

2. Do I have old resentments I can let go of?

3. How can I suggest other words someone could say to make their point without hurting my feelings or making me mad?

4. How can I make a better choice than my typical angry reaction?

Hadley: When you find your answers and take action on them, you break through an angry rut and shake things up in positive ways. This improves your interactions with everyone in your life.

Which of these 8 tools do most breakup survivors resist?

While breakup emotions are raw and intense, many people resist using Tool Number 7: Forgive, but don't forget. Let's make sure that you make a better choice next...

6.

Love Test - Will You Forgive, Or Let That Old Grudge Kill You?

This is a wake up call for anyone who refuses to forgive wrongdoers. You may suffer serious, even fatal consequences, if you fail to do the emotional work needed to pass life's toughest Love Tests, like these:

How do you forgive the unfaithful?

Could you ever forgive yourself for a crime of passion, or for a loss of passion that may have killed your relationship?

Why should you forgive dishonesty, abuse, infidelity, or the theft of your trust, love, hopes and dreams?

You forgive, because "unforgiveness" is the poison that destroys your own health, happiness and relationships.

What if you refuse to forgive someone's offenses?

They don't suffer. You do. You hand yourself over to other torturers--namely experiences of fear, depression, frustration, anxiety, bitterness, self-hatred, disease and loneliness.

Learning how to forgive had saved my life during my divorce. As I'd admitted earlier, I had been filled with unforgiveness, anger and blame that had made my heart feel ready to explode.

How did I change that?

I learned how to forgive my former husband and myself for ways we'd hurt each other during the breakup of our marriage. I'll show you my radical forgiveness technique in the next chapter.

But first, I'll give you medical incentive to get good at forgiveness:

If you don't forgive, that old grudge can kill you. How?

Having hostility pumping through your veins releases stress hormones. It can shut down your immune system, leave you vulnerable to disease, and make you unable to eat or sleep, or overindulge in both.

If harboring resentment continues for long periods of time, you can wire your brain to form an unforgiving, hostile world view. This can destroy your body and your relationships, because no one wants to be around unforgiving, angry people.

What's the common reason people refuse to forgive?

People think forgiveness condones hurtful behavior. This is not true. Forgiveness is a process of coping with an offense, so you don't allow it to harm you.

Unforgiveness often causes more harm than the original offense that hurt you, in ways I've just explained.

What's your healthier choice?

You break the bond of unforgiveness, before it breaks you. How?

Use this step-by-step guide to forgive even the most egregious offenses, which I've summarized from my radio interview for A Lasting Love with Dr. Juliet Rohde-Brown.

She is a psychologist, a world-renowned teacher of forgiveness and author of Imagine Forgiveness: How To Create A Joyful Future.

Hadley: Let's clear up any confusion about what it means to forgive. How do you define forgiveness?

Dr. Juliet: Forgiveness is a process that is clearly defined by researchers Enright and Fitzgibbons, who have run clinical studies on how people forgive:

"People upon rationally determining that they've been unfairly treated, forgive when they willfully abandon resentment and related responses to which they have a right, and endeavor to respond to the wrongdoer based on the moral principle of beneficence-- which may include compassion, unconditional worth, generosity and moral love to which the wrongdoer, by nature of the hurtful act or acts, has no right."

Hadley: I've got a question about beneficence, which refers to an act that benefits others. Doesn't forgiveness benefit the one who forgives even more than their wrongdoer?

Dr. Juliet: It depends on the model of forgiveness, whether it's for learning or reconciliation. You can forgive someone without informing them, so that you reap the

25

health benefits. If you actually reconcile with your wrongdoer, then each of you benefit.

Hadley: When someone has a serious offense to forgive, what steps do they take to go through the forgiveness process?

Dr. Juliet: I suggest you take these steps to forgiveness:

* Start with an uncovering what it is that you want to forgive.

* Make a decision to forgive. This sounds like, "I decide to forgive so-and-so for such-and-such." You fill in the person's name and offense. Use your own name, if you want to forgive yourself.

* Begin the work phase. Do some practices like mindfulness, loving kindness, journaling and possibly working with a therapist to help you forgive the worst offenses. You lead with your core values, which helps you rise above any offense and be more mature by doing so.

* Notice how the process deepens your sense of self and changes your perspective on the world. When you make a difference in yourself, you make a difference in the world. It's not an easy process, but it works.

Hadley: Do you follow the same process, if you want to forgive yourself for something you've done or failed to do?

Dr. Juliet: When we forgive ourselves, we must add another step to this forgiveness process. We need to achieve reconciliation with ourselves.

We do this by coming back to a place of loving ourselves, of treating ourselves like a responsible parent treats a helpless child, who depends on them.

We protect, embrace, feed and nurture our innocent child inside our core. We keep them warm and safe from things that can go wrong. When we reconcile with ourselves, we reconcile with that innocent part--with the child, who has a sense of wonder in the world

Hadley: Will you suggest an exercise to help us reconcile and reconnect with our innocence?

Dr. Juliet: One way to do it is to work with mindfulness practices. First, you get into an awareness stance, being aware of your breathing and thoughts passing.

Then do the loving kindness meditation by taking these 5 steps:

1. You envision yourself as a young child with big, innocent eyes looking out at you. While breathing deeply from your belly, you see your own face in front of you, and you offer love to your younger self.

2. Next you move your imagined image to someone, whom it's very easy to love and feel their love in return. This person can be living, deceased, an imaginary person, even an animal. You see their face in front of you, and you open your heart to give love back and forth.

3. Then you move into images of loving family or friends. When you get used to making a heart connection with them, then you are ready for the next step.

4. Look at an image of someone, who is causing you to struggle. Then extend loving kindness to them.

5. Go back to imagining someone, who is easy to love. Then repeat the process.

Hadley: What are some proven benefits of the loving kindness exercise?

Dr. Juliet: As you do this exercise, you feel loving kindness in its purity. This creates a shift in your body away from the tense clenching of unforgiveness, into the calm peace of forgiveness.

When you do this exercise on a regular basis, it also helps you make a heart connection with people you see in your daily life. This deepens and enriches your relationships.

Hadley: Einstein had said that imagination is more important than knowledge. Through imagination, you use all of your senses to learn and to change your life and the lives of everyone around you. So how do we use our imagination as a bridge into forgiveness?

Dr. Juliet: Do this exercise to get into your body and duplicate the stressful sensations of unforgiveness. Then instantly replace them with calm feelings of forgiveness:

* Tighten and clench every part of your body, which shows you what you're doing to yourself when you don't forgive.

* After you tighten up, then you let it go. Take a deep breath to release tension, and then start breathing through your belly to ground yourself in calm feelings.

* Now turn your thoughts to the most joyful moment in your life. See it, remember the smells, tastes, sounds or physical touch. Use your senses to re-experience the delight you'd felt in that joyful moment.

* Experience joy in other ways, like going out in nature for walks. Take a rock and throw it into the stream as you say to yourself, "I let this go."

It is that easy for some people to let go of something they want to forgive. It's more difficult for most of us and may require daily practice of taking each step in the forgiveness process that we've explained.

Hadley: Tell us how forgiveness affects other people in your life.

Dr. Juliet: Researchers have measured the effects of forgiveness in the person doing the forgiving and in the people around them.

Forgiveness not only lifts your spirits and helps you radiate joy, it also has the same effect in other people who spend time with you.

We have scientific proof that our emotional and spiritual energy is contagious. You have the power to experience and scatter joy, when you practice forgiveness.

Hadley: So it's important to know that forgiveness is not about condoning hurtful behavior. It is not about going back into an abusive relationship.

It is about expecting integrity and honorable behavior from people.

It's about calling them on wrongdoing and using the forgiveness process to protect your own health and happiness, and improve the quality of your life and relationships.

Earlier, I'd promised to tell you about the radical forgiveness technique that had helped me stop being the victim and start being the creator of a great new life.

You do this by making shifts in your thinking, which you discover next…

7.

Radical Forgiveness - Why You Can't Make Mistakes In Relationships

Back to my story. As you may recall, I had been tormented by the anger of unforgiveness for months during my divorce. Blaming my husband and myself for mistakes that caused our breakup had made my heart feel ready to explode.

I'd needed emergency relief. I'd found it, as soon as I made these shifts in my thinking:

Shift 1. You can't make mistakes in a relationship. You only make choices with love lessons attached like a bow.

How do you identify a love lesson in each choice?

Let's say you'd entered a relationship with someone, who withholds affection or criticizes you the same way one of your childhood caregivers did.

Your love lesson in this choice might be, "I wanted to win the love from someone as illusive or critical as my parent."

Can you think of another love lesson in this example, or in your own love story?
Jot down your choices and love lessons to complete Shift --1. Then make--

Shift 2. Learn the love lessons, so you don't have to repeat them in a new relationship.

In our example above, you observe your pattern or reason you were attracted to a withholding or critical partner, like a parent or caregiver.

To learn your love lesson in your choice, you might say to yourself:

"I won't bang my head against that wall again." Or, "I'm done with that choice. I'm free to choose a new partner, who will love me how I deserve to be loved."

Remember your love lessons and make daily choices to learn from joy. A joyful choice is:

Shift 3. Give thanks to your greatest teachers for giving you the lessons you needed to learn in that moment, to grow into a wiser, more loving YOU.

Why do you give silent thanks for people or circumstances that trigger your pain?

Because they show you patterns or habits you need to break, so you find and fulfill your purpose and get all the love and happiness you deserve. This builds the foundation for:

Shift 4. With this new attitude and with gratitude for your love lessons learned, you have no one to blame and nothing to forgive.

The burden of blame and unforgiveness vanishes, as you make these 4
shifts. Why?
It's because you:
* See every challenging person or circumstance in your life as a catalyst for growth and change

* Appreciate how they help you see and heal parts of yourself that need healing

* Feel thankful that you've empowered yourself to replace old patterns with better choices that create the life and relationships you love.

When I'd made these shifts in my thinking, I'd developed a new attitude that had eased my anger against my former husband and myself. This freed me to create a graceful divorce and remain friendly co-parents to our children, who now are happily launched.

This new attitude frees you to start fresh and love again, even better than before. It improves all of your interactions with your former partner, and builds even better relationships with family and friends, co-workers and colleagues, and with a new intimate partner someday.

I encourage you to make these shifts in your thinking and practice the other forgiveness exercises that you've just discovered. See how good it feels to stop being the victim and start being the creator of your best new life.

When will you be ready to create a happy, new love story?

Let's make sure your sad, old love stories aren't a barrier to new love next…

8.

Write A Happy, New Ending To A Sad, Old Love Story - Without Lying

Are your sad, old love stories stopping you from creating happy, new ones? Find out, by taking this simple Love Test.

When you're asked about a past relationship, do you:

* Tell the same old story of its troubles and unhappy ending?

* Explain the disappointments or betrayals that lead to a bad break up?

* Describe all the ways you're still struggling to get over it?

* Mention all the reasons that subsequent relationships haven't worked out?

* Talk about difficult obstacles in your current relationships?

* Complain that your love life isn't working out the way you'd liked?

How did you score?

Each NO response reveals where you've grown through the pain of lost love and you've learned your lessons from loss. Now you get a happiness boost, when you write a happy ending to your old love stories.

Each YES response reveals where your sad, old stories are stopping you from creating happy, new ones. How do you break through this barrier to new love?

Write A Happy Ending To Your Sad Old Love Story Without Lying In 3 Steps:

Step 1. Rewrite your past.

When you face troubling events in life or in a relationship, you have an emotional reaction to them. You tell yourself stories to ease your pain or place the blame on someone else.

The more often you tell these sad stories, the deeper they get wired into your brain and become an automatic monologue that you keep repeating.

It's a sad, old monologue that nobody wants to hear. People tune you out or disappear from your life, until you rewrite your sad, old stories with some happy, new endings.

How do you do this without lying to yourself and others? Take the next two steps.

Step 2. Remember the love.

When you look back at your life, see through the eyes of love instead of fear. The popular acronym for FEAR is False Events Appearing Real. Fear is a false story that taints your view of the past, because only love is real.

It is your choice to live in love or in fear. How do you choose love?

You choose which of your thoughts, memories, beliefs and stories you tell yourself and others. That's hard to accept, while you're gripped by many forms of fear. You may recognize fear as anger, jealousy, sarcasm, addiction to food, drugs, limiting beliefs or any form of self-defeating behavior that blocks love.

Your heart doesn't speak the language of fear. Your Ego does. How do you tame your fearful ego?

You rewrite a fearful story or memory with a loving ending. When you are willing and eager to do this, you are in the right mindset for the next step.

Step 3. Focus on the beauty you want to experience again.

A universal law states that what you focus on expands. You get more of what you focus on, so take control of your focus. Stop focusing on what you don't want. Focus exclusively on what you do want, so you bring more of it into your life.

What if you can't shift your focus? What if you are stuck in a sad, old story?

Take a few deep breaths. Say, FEAR, to yourself. Then self correct by taking these steps:

*Look for the love lessons you may learn from that experience. Now learn them, so you don't have to repeat them again.

*Uncover the silver lining in the dark cloud of each troubling experience, memory, story. And give thanks for it.

*Talk about the beauty of loving moments and memories that you want to experience again. Because you will.

When you take these steps each consecutive day for only 2-3 weeks, you create a new

Love Habit and a new Love Story that replace the old ones.

As you see your past and present through the eyes of love and you speak from your heart, you create an honest happy ending to your sad, old love stories. And you free yourself to create happy new ones.

I know how challenging it can be to free yourself from the clutches of fear. This is a critical step to end heartbreak. So let's make sure you get all the help you need to transform fear into love next...

3 / What if you feel ready to start dating and creating a happy, new love story? Let's be sure you don't waste valuable time dating the wrong people. Discover 7 new ways to find great people to date, love and marry in my gift e-book when you visit www.IFindLoveFast.com

9.
Turning Fear and Loneliness Into Love In 2 Steps

A bad breakup often causes two side effects. You may feel less desirable and more afraid of being alone or lonely for the rest of your life. These fears linger and sabotage your recovery, until you use this proven 2-step remedy:

1. Face Your Fears

Many newly-single men and women escape the fear of being alone with pain killers, like alcohol, pharmaceuticals, over working, over-eating, over-sleeping, over-dating.

Numbing your fears can't release them.   Facing your fears helps you find a path out of them. Need help to identify your fears?

Let's consider some possibilities. Are you afraid of:

* sleeping alone
* eating alone
* staying stuck in painful emotions
* denying your dreams of travel
* facing health challenges alone
* losing chances to be appreciated
* shutting down your sexual desires
* growing old, without experiencing intimacy or romance again
* searching but not finding a love match as wonderful as your former love
* creating debt, instead of building wealth
* raising children alone, as a single parent
* feeling isolated from married friends
* being stuck in a dead-end job or directionless dating
* feeling drained of energy and enthusiasm, with no way to recharge your joyful vitality

What other fears can you think of?

Jot them down now. Then take the next step.

2. Use The Right Remedy To Relieve Each Fear

Once you've listed your fears, you are ready to use the best remedy to ease each fear.

Fortunately, a single remedy often eases many fears at once. This is it:

Whatever you're lacking, you give it and it's gone.

Whatever you fear you're missing out on, whatever you're afraid you won't receive from someone else, you simply give this to yourself. Feelings of lack disappear, as soon as you fulfill your own needs, wants, and desires.

How do you apply this remedy?

Consider the following fears and the best remedies to release them:

Feeling unappreciated and unloved?
Find ways to express hearty appreciation and love to yourself every day.

Feeling disconnected from former friends or buried dreams?
Reach out and make connections with new single friends for dining, travel, seminars, book discussions or courses. This helps you fulfill your dreams of even greater friendship, fun, health, fitness, wealth, success, happiness and love.

Feeling stuck on your ex or destructive emotions?
Take positive steps each day to let go of the past and start fresh with a positive attitude and action plan.

How is this process working for you thus far?

What gets measured gets improved, so let's measure your progress next...

10.
Love Test - 8 Sure-Fire Signs That You're Over Your Ex

Want to know for sure that you are over your ex? If so, ask yourself these 8 questions:

1. Does your ex no longer occupy your thoughts constantly?

2. Have you stopped thinking about what could've happened, or what you could've said or done to save your past relationship?

3. Have you stopped getting upset with your ex, so that you now remain calm in your dealings with each other?

4. Have you stopped trying to please or doing favors for your ex?

5. Have you stopped talking about your ex with your friends?

6. Have you let go of romantic feelings and stopped having breakup sex?

7. Do you no longer feel jealous that your ex is involved with someone new?

8. Do you feel positive about yourself and your future, no matter what your ex thinks or says about you?

How did you score?

If you answered YES to all 8 questions, congratulations!
You've done the emotional work necessary to detach emotionally from your former partner. You've broken up with your past love and freed yourself to fall in love again, with yourself and your new life.

What if you answered NO to one or more of these questions?
Each NO response shows you where you still need to detach, forgive, or wrap up unfinished business with your former partner. You need resilience, optimism and discipline to let go of your old life with your ex and use new remedies and love skills to build the life and relationships you love now.

Have you tried these remedies, but failed to get the relief you desire?

Consider adding a shocking remedy to your healing regimen next...

11.

Shocking Remedy Solves Love Problems Fast

Let's look to mathematics for a lovely reminder of the universal law of polarity, which states that every problem has a solution built into it. Too often we give up on a problem before finding the solution, which is the gift of the problem.

Why is it a gift?

Because finding the solution to problems is how you keep growing in life and love. When a problem arises, you give thanks for the chance to find the solution that keeps you growing and becoming the person you're meant to be.

What's the best way to find solutions to tough problems?

I'd like you to consider a transformational concept that is known only by the elite one to three percent of people alive today, although it was known by great teachers and thought leaders throughout history.

You may be as shocked by this concept as I was, when I tell you how I found out about it. If you use it, you may be amazed by how fast it helps you transform your life with love.

What is this life-changing concept?

Before I reveal it, I'll lay the foundation to help you understand it. Einstein said that we can't solve problems using the same thinking that created them. Carl Jung said that we never solve our problems, we just learn to outgrow them. How?

You grow to great heights when you use a different way of thinking to produce different results. Einstein explained how he and other great thinkers did this when he said, "I only want to think like God thinks. The rest is details."

The good news is you don't have to be an Einstein to do this. You think like God thinks, as soon as you become aware of a great, astonishing truth that empowers you to create the life you love.

What is this astonishing truth?

You are the Great I Am. You are an expression of the divine, a human manifestation of God.

This concept used to be considered heresy when, in the name of God, women and men had been condemned as heretics, tortured and even burned at the stake by the church, simply because they believed in our personal connection with God. This idea was revolutionary at that time.

Today, you won't be persecuted for believing in your intimate connection with God, or for believing how your Great I Am empowers you to achieve great things and experience great love in your daily life.

What's your gut reaction to this idea? Doubt? Belief? Shock?

If you doubt this, that makes you feel as if you lack love. How do you change doubt into belief?

You acknowledge your inner source of infinite love and possibilities. And you become aware of the truths that great thinkers have been telling us throughout history:

* God is the place of well being, from which you came and to which you will return.
* God is your inner source of infinite energy and love, that is present in each moment. God is always present in the now, so in the present moment you connect with source energy.
* In God, all things are possible, so any thoughts that you can't do or be something are of your ego--not of God.
* God speaks to you in feelings of joyful passion, while you're doing something you love. You are God manifested, so you have no limitations, except those you choose to believe.

What do you believe?

If you're like me, you were not raised to believe this. I was raised a Catholic and trained to believe that God was out there. So we needed a Priest to connect with God, while he administered the sacraments.

We did get the chance to "be one with God" during mass, while we swallowed a communion wafer and said prayers. As soon as mass ended, we went back to being separated from our divine, infinite source of love.

I'd believed that this separation was real until my late teens, when I had a wake-up call that had raised my love awareness. It happened while I was in college, soon after my grandmother had died. I'd loved her more than anyone, so I was devastated by her death.

A few nights after her funeral, I woke up feeling freezing cold in my college room. As I opened my eyes, I saw my grandmother, sitting there in her rocking chair, smiling at me.

I'd asked her my first question that came to mind. "Is there a God?"

"God is the spirit of perfection inside each of us."

Her news had shocked me, because she'd been a devout Catholic and what she'd revealed was a radical concept of God. When I'd reached out to hug her, she'd vanished.

Yet through her brief visit, she'd left me with a new awareness of my personal relationship with the divine.

Her appearance had illustrated how energy neither can be created nor destroyed, it only changes forms, even after physical death. She'd launched my spiritual search for even greater awareness of our connection with divine love.

A couple years ago, I'd told this story to my dinner date, who had won a Nobel Prize in physics.

"You conjured up your grandmother to feel better," he'd said.

"How could I conjure up a new idea about God, if I didn't know it at that time? Did I get a tip from the collective consciousness? Is God a shapeshifter, who appears in a form I recognize to heal my grief?"

He'd shrugged and told me again that I'd conjured up my conversation with my dead grandmother. I'd lacked proof to argue the point. So the truth remains a mystery.

Yet the ancient and modern wisdom I've studied since college seems to reinforce what I'd first learned from my grandmother's visit after her death:

That the spirit of perfection, the infinite source of love and possibility, is inside each of us. That we are God manifested, so we have infinite, limitless power to create the life we love.

Doubt this?

That may be why you keep yearning and searching for love. To become open to this truth, you may need a wake up call, like a tragic loss, a serious conflict or a great challenge. Why?

In times of great loss or great challenges, the resulting pain opens the doorway to the spiritual and creative realms. When you take this path out of pain, you become open to raising your love awareness and thinking like God thinks.

Accept this?

Then you instantly find great love and feel empowered to greatness, by tapping into your inner source of infinite love.

You attract even more love, because a universal law states that you attract more of what you are, not what you want.

Another universal law states that what you focus on expands. I often say that what you think about, you bring about. So choose your thoughts wisely.

When you choose to think like God thinks in your daily practice, you tap into your infinite power to heal heartbreak and return to your natural state of joy, by living a life of kindness, passion, happiness and love.

Need a nudge?

Find out what the world's Love Luminaries think about this idea in the next chapter…

12.

Feel Loved and Happy, No Matter Who Is Or Isn't Sleeping Beside You

One hundred fifty of the world's Love Luminaries were interviewed by Marci Shimoff for her latest best-selling book, Love For No Reason. Marci reveals how you find love from the inside, no matter who's missing or what life throws you, in highlights of our radio conversation for A Lasting Love.

Marci Shimoff is a former PBS-TV host, a writer, who's sold 14 million books as a co-author of Chicken Soup For The Woman's Soul, and the author of Happy For No Reason. Now she helps you feel loved and happy for no reason.

Hadley: The moment I met you during a speaking engagement, I could see that you radiated love, like the sun beaming from your heart. So it's clear that you practice the Love Habits, which you write about in Love For No Reason. Many people want more love in life, yet they don't know how to get it. Tell us why the concept of getting love is false, and what we can do instead.

Marci: Most of us have been trained to think of love as a stream of energy that goes between two people. We think, "I'm going to get love and give love in this relationship."

This limiting view of love makes us Love Beggars, always asking for love. What's missing is the reality that we are love. Truth is, we are the ocean of love, and we are overflowing with love.

Trusting this naturally makes you a Love Philanthropist. You don't go looking for love in all the wrong places, when you know you are love. And you've got plenty of love to give away.

Hadley: You've interviewed 150 of world's love luminaries to get their advice for your new book. Yet I sense you've made the breakthrough discovery. Tell us how you identified our "Love Body."

Marci: I realized that all 150 love experts shared a definition of love for no reason, which is an internal state of love that doesn't depend on a person or situation or romantic partner. It's being love, rather than getting love.

I noticed these common characteristics of living in this state of love:

* Being grounded and fully present in each moment.

* Being okay with feeling your feelings, allowing sadness or other feelings to flow through you.

* Moving through life with an open heart filled with gratitude and forgiveness.

Our Love Luminaries all said that we connect with feeling love and being love, when we activate all 7 energy centers (chakras). Then the energy of love flows freely in our body.

I called this our "Love Body." We strengthen it by listening to messages of intuition, which are generated from the heart. Scientists at Heart Math Institute have measured the heart's energy field, which extends 7 feet away from the body.

Hadley: And our heart's intuition picks up insights even faster than our brain, according to Heart Math studies. The heart's intuition is sensed in the whisper of your inner voice, so it's wise to listen for the whisper of insight and take action on it.

I'm curious how you were able to write this book about finding love and being love, while you were going through difficult challenges with your husband, Sergio.

Marci: Writers are told to watch what you write about, because you certainly will be tested on it. As soon as I signed my contract to write Love For No Reason, my husband and I decided to divorce.

It's hard to go through a divorce and keep your heart open. As I interviewed each Love Luminary for my book, I practiced what everyone told me, and it worked for me. As the pain of divorce came up, I felt the pain and let it go.

I also recognized that my husband wasn't the source of my love; he was just the trigger. I was able to find the source of true love in myself using the same exercises you find in Love For No Reason.

Hadley: Most of us need help getting through our greatest challenges with an open heart. How do we feel loved and happy, despite our outer circumstances?

Marci: I'll give you three exercises from my book, so you can choose your favorite.

First, I'd like you to do this Heart Math exercise three times a day for two weeks, so it becomes a new Love Habit:

Place your hand over your heart. This starts the release of oxytocin -- the love and bonding hormone.

Imagine you are breathing in and out through your heart.

Picture your breath coming in and out through center of your heart. It doesn't matter if you see it, or feel it, or which sense you use to breathe through your heart.

Breathe in ease and compassion and love on every inhale. Then exhale normally.

Again, inhale love through your heart, repeating the process for a couple minutes.

If you do this exercise once, you may feel soothed, grounded and open hearted.

If you do this exercise a few times each day, you place your body in the Love Response. As soon as you place your hand on your heart, you feel love washing over you.

Hadley: According to a Harvard Study, the Love Response allows your body to adapt to challenges, reverse disease, maintain health and improve, rather than deteriorate with age. So we've all got incentive to love for no reason. Yet we also block the flow of love through criticism, limiting beliefs, judgments or fears. What exercise breaks through these love blocks?

Marci: You can't have a great experience of love, until you are loving to yourself. You use this exercise in self love to care for yourself and open your heart to love:

Three times each day, stop and ask yourself this question: What's the most loving thing I can do for myself right now?

The answer might be getting a glass of water or some fresh air. Or stop beating up on yourself, and acknowledge your good qualities, and focus on gratitude.

If we don't pay attention to our own self care, then we aren't being loving with ourselves. The way we treat the world is a mirror of how we treat ourselves. So do this exercise three times per day to create a new Love Habit of loving yourself.

Hadley: To clarify, we're not talking about self love that is selfish, but healthy self love that promotes your well being and that of everyone around you.

Marci: And if you're a parent, the best thing you can do for your children is to raise your own experience of love, so you model it for them. Your emotions are contagious, and your children catch your emotions. Let them catch your love, instead of fear, anger and stress.

Hadley: We want to be around people who are loving, and we want to run from people who are angry and stressed. So how do we fast track more love into our life?

Marci: The quickest way to feel more love and happiness is through forgiveness. You can't feel love, if you're holding onto grudges.

Hadley: Unforgiveness is like swallowing poison and expecting someone else to die. The antidote is forgiveness. What technique do you recommend?

Marci: My favorite forgiveness technique is from the Kahuna Hawaiian tradition. It involves thinking of the person or act that has hurt you, and feeling these four phrases in your heart:

I'm sorry
Please forgive me
Thank you
I love you

It doesn't matter who the offender is. You simply sit with your eyes closed for a few minutes and think of person or incident that you need to forgive.

As you feel each phrase, you enter their name or your own name, if you need to forgive yourself for something you did or failed to do.

Do this forgiveness exercise a few times every day for a couple weeks, because the experience of love is about creating new Love Habits. So pick one of these three exercises and practice it three times a day for the next two weeks to form a new Love Habit.

Hadley: I'd like to clarify that you are not actually addressing your wrongdoer when you say and feel these four phrases. Imagine that you are speaking to your higher power, with the purpose of releasing painful experiences from your past and cleansing these traumas from your memory bank. This cleanses pain and reverses dis-ease it may have triggered in you.

This Hawaiian healing exercise also frees you to feel the infinite source of love flowing inside you. Since you attract what you are, not what you want, you attract even more love, like a love magnet, after you dispose of unforgiveness.

Why do so many of us have to hit bottom before we use these love skills to bounce back from setbacks and build the life we love?

Get the answers and the antidotes in the next chapter...

13.
Bouncing Back From Setbacks In 5 Steps

Here's good news for involuntary singles, who've lost someone they love; for employees, who've been downsized out of a job; and for anyone who wants to end heartbreak and bounce back quickly from the toughest setbacks.

You make a magical recovery from any loss and make your life even better than ever with success tools that you gain in highlights of my radio interview for A Lasting Love with Donna Marie Thompson, Ph.D.

Dr. Donna wrote the bestselling book, Bouncing Back From Loss: How To Learn From Your Past, Build The Present and Transform Your Future.

Hadley: Why do so many of us have to hit bottom, while grieving a loss, before we look for a path out of pain?

Dr. Donna: The lowest level of energy is being the victim of a loss. Getting stuck in the victim way of thinking actually drains your energy, so you can't pull yourself out of it.

Hadley: When I was on my knees in grief after the tragic loss of my marriage, I eventually found relief in this Sufi saying:

"When the heart grieves over what it has lost, the spirit rejoices over what it has left."

Giving thanks for the love and blessings that remain in your life creates more feelings of love and gratitude. This lifts you up from your knees. How do you help people shift from grief to gratitude and love?

Dr. Donna: I help people end heartbreak and bounce back from loss by using 5 steps, which I call my 5 E's:

1. Explore what happened, by writing in your journal.

The more you unload in your journaling, the less emotional weight you carry.

2. Eliminate unwanted feelings.

You may have no idea that you can control your feelings. But you can let go of painful feelings and choose feelings that support and strengthen you. It's your choice.

You can set time boundaries for grieving a certain number of hours each day, and stick to it. If you're angry, decide how much time you'll spend each day being angry. As soon as you reach your daily quota, then move on to other emotions and actions.

This is a gradual process that lets people have their grief and angry feelings, but limit them. You discover it's your life and your time, so why will you devote all your energy to thoughts and feelings that drag you down?

If you need help in the beginning, seek counseling or medication from an M.D. Keep the faith that, "This too shall pass."

3. Embrace the situation.

Accept that, "What Is IS."

Looking back at the past and thinking, "What if" and "If only," actually serves no purpose, except wasting your time.

4. Envision your new future.

Start shedding even more of your past, that you'd planned before your loss.

Realize that you now can make new choices, which change the course of your life.

Stop seeing what you've lost, and start seeing all that you have.

5. Energize your present opportunities and help others do the same.

Shifting your focus away from yourself and toward helping others is a great healer of grief.

Hadley: What if you can't seem to help others or build the life you love? What if you're stuck in the clutches of destructive behavior that steals joy and sabotages love?

Let's break through those barriers to even greater love and happiness next...

14.

4-Step Proven Cure To Tough Addictions, Including Sex and Drugs

What if you could take 4 steps to end the toughest addictions, including sex, drugs, gambling, workaholism or any form of negative thinking and acting?

What if you could use a $20 book to end obsessive behaviors and save yourself $20,000 in therapy, when you follow this advice?

You may turn these "what if's" into reality, by using the 4-step addiction cure that you discover in highlights of my radio interview for A Lasting Love with Dr. Winn Henderson.

Dr. Winn is a retired physician, radio host, author of Freedom From Addiction plus 37 other books, which promote optimal health and happiness.

Hadley: You claim that your addiction cure has a 100 percent success rate. How did you develop and test your program to end tough addictions?

Dr. Winn: I was an ER doctor, who'd treated thousands of trauma cases, and I observed that most of these injuries were related to addictions. I concluded that if we could get rid of addictions, we could end the cause of a lot of pain and suffering.

So I researched addiction treatments used from 1935 onward, and I found them costly and ineffective.

Then I formulated my own treatment plan, and I tested it on thousands of patients.

We had a 100 percent success rate when patients had one common trait -- the strong desire to be free of the addiction.

Hadley: So it's essential to have a strong desire to release addictive behavior, before starting this program. Tell us how to take these 4 steps.

Dr. Winn: First step is to identify your problem. If you keep doing something that hurts yourself or your loved ones, and you can't seem to stop this behavior, then you are addicted.

You may not want to accept this is a problem, because you get a rush of pleasure from it that you don't want to give up.

Some addictions, like sexual addiction, often can be hidden from your partner, when you conduct your affairs in secrecy. You may deny you have a problem by thinking, "Everyone in my world does this."

You can't hide it forever. Eventually, your problem will become apparent to your loved ones or to the world, if you are a public figure like Tiger Woods. This is when the pain of your addiction outweighs the pleasure of pursuing it.

Hadley: I've found that pain opens the doorway to personal growth. Pain is your wake up call for positive action, like taking these 4 steps. What's next?

Dr. Winn: Your second step is to find your answers to 4 spiritual questions:

Who am I?
Where did I come from?
What am I doing here?
Where am I going, when I'm done?

You don't need therapy to answer these questions. You can sit down with my book, and I'll help you find your answers.

The most important question to answer for an addiction cure is, "What am I doing here?"

This question helps you find your purpose in life and identify obstacles that stop you from fulfilling it, so that you can overcome them. With a strong life purpose, you don't take detours down destructive paths.

Hadley: How else do we stay on a constructive path?

Dr. Winn: Your third step is to believe in the program. Commit that you will do whatever it takes to solve your problem. Take correct action every day to replace destructive habits with constructive, positive actions.

Your forth step is to focus on your life purpose. A lack of spiritual understanding and a lack of mission in life cause you to crave fulfillment in harmful ways.

When you find the answers to these four spiritual questions and you fulfill your life purpose, then you no longer crave fulfillment in ways that hurt you and the people you love.

Hadley: The Dalai Lama says that the best way to cure an addiction is to replace that behavior with something better. Let's compare your 4-step program with conventional treatment. In your program, do sexoholics have to give up sex to end their sex addiction, like alcoholics have to give up alcohol?

Dr. Winn: Alcoholics don't have to give up alcohol forever, when they focus on fulfilling their life purpose every day. An unwavering commitment to fulfilling your life mission also helps sex addicts stop their destructive habit and form a healthy sexual relationship.

Hadley: Finding answers to the Four Questions may help you release addictive behaviors, thoughts, feelings or limiting beliefs, and then replace them with something better. This frees you to fulfill your life purpose, which brings you all the happiness you deserve.

Are you conjuring up reasons why you can't replace self-defeating habits with better ones and build the life you love?

You break through these barriers to even greater love, success and happiness, when you design your ideal future next...

15.
Creating The Future You Love Now

Do you ever blame your current problems on past circumstances?

Do you ever think you'd be even happier in life and love, if only you'd had a happier childhood, better role models, a better education or job?

Have you ever sabotaged love and marriage, or settled for a dull, frustrating love life?

If you answered YES to any question, you may put that behind you now. You enrich your life and relationships, by using a newly-trademarked technique.

This is not the outdated techniques that you may have used before, without success. This is not more "Affirmations", "Positive Thinking" or telling you to just "Be In the Moment" because "Everything Happens for a Reason".

This is about developing a relationship with Your Future Self. No doctor, healer, coach, or seminar can teach you the Future Visioning tm Process for tapping into the Incredible Power of The Future, because this process of working with the future has never been available before.

Discover how to use this radical, new technique to quickly heal your past, in highlights of my radio interview for A Lasting Love with Ti Caine. He is the leading expert on the psychology of the future and the creator of the Future Visioning Process tm.

Hadley: Let's help people get unstuck from emotional pain, unhappiness and frustration in life and relationships. We may have tried talk therapy, affirmations or mood-altering pharmaceuticals, which failed to bring the joy, success, health and love we all deserve.

You claim that your new process quickly and powerfully heals your past and creates a great future. Does it really work? If so, how?

Ti: Not only does it work, it's the only thing that ever has worked. Creating the future is literally what we are doing every moment of our lives. Yet most of us don't know it.

If you're not conscious of creating the future you want, then you create a repetition of your past.

Hadley: Many people blame past circumstances for their current problems. How do you help us change that?

Ti: First, I explain that if you don't consciously choose your future, then your parents already have.

Hadley: Because of childhood programming, or watching and modeling our parents' frustrating relationships?

Ti: Both. In childhood, we see what adult life looks like. I've never met anyone who came from a perfectly-functional family. So we grow up and develop some derivative of our parents' lives.

The average person is programmed for mediocrity, for a difficult, painful life that ends in an ugly, disempowered death. That's what our parents lived, what our society predicts, and for what most of us are programmed.

Hadley: So we need to reprogram ourselves to create the future we want. What's the first step?

Ti: First, you must understand that you are living a future that was programmed into you, not for you or by you. So first, you recognize the problem is in the future, not in the past.

Yet, using this process lets you go back and heal past issues quickly. Remember the problem is not behind us; it's in front of us. We live our way into the future every day.

Hadley: Understanding this helps us leave old baggage in the past, where it belongs. Let's assume we want to change outdated programming and create a future that's better than our past. How do we start the process?

Ti: Some people do it naturally. About one to three percent of people may have been born being future oriented, because they are naturally happier, healthier and more successful, without knowing how they do this. They just know what their future looks like, because it works naturally.

Most of us were programmed for love and life that doesn't work. If you don't change that, you continue to create that and stay on the track that's heading for a wall.

I've studied all the other therapies in the past 40 years, and they're all equivalent to re-arranging the deck chairs on the Titanic.

Unless you change the course of the Titanic, it doesn't matter what else you do -- positive thinking or talking about your past in therapy, or how many affirmations you write, or Law of Attraction stuff that you do. If you don't go out and change the future first, then everything else is literally a waste of time.

Hadley: So we must change course, choose our ideal course, before we create the future we want. Tell us the best steps to take right now.

Ti: Step 1 is to design your ideal future, where your dreams come true in all areas of your life, including relationships, health, finances, career, friendships, relationships, spirituality.

Hadley: I encourage my online community to design your ideal love life, as if there are no barriers, no obstacles to stop you from reaching your peak of love and getting all the happiness you deserve now.

Ti: This is your best strategy because, as the French philosopher said, "We are spiritual beings having a human experience, not human beings having a spiritual experience."

Because we are spiritual beings, we have an infinite source of power to create the life we want. Quantum physics has proven that we literally create our own reality through our thoughts.

Hadley: What you think about, you bring about. You start creating your ideal reality by thinking about what your life will be like when all your dreams come true. Then write it down, to make it real.

Here are some Future Visioning writing guidelines to help you design the life you love:

* How will you feel emotionally, while living your ideal future? Describe how you will enjoy and express your full range of emotions, while living your ideal life.

* Describe your ideal loving relationship and/or family. Include specific qualities for you and your mate. Describe the size of your family, the relationships between members and a list of aspirations, including things you would like to do together.

*Visualize a totally fulfilling social life. Describe the friends, business associates and community acquaintances you will enjoy, including the social events and the position or image you want to attain. Whatever you imagine, list it.

* Describe your ideal physical and health state, weight, nutrition, exercise patterns and the activities you would like to be involved in, as part of an energetic and joyful life.

* Describe the mental state you want to attain, including all of the things you'd like to learn and know, the creativity you would like to develop, the formal and informal education level you would like to achieve, and the things that turn you on intellectually.

* What do you want in your life career-wise and financially three to five years from now? How will you feel in your ideal career? Imagine your financial dreams coming true. Be specific and list anything of value that would be symbolic of financial success, especially your giving.

* What do you really want in your life spiritually in three to five years? Describe the spiritual and moral state to which you aspire. Describe how you feel, as if you've already accomplished all of this.

Hadley: Now that you are fulfilling your vision for your best life, I will fulfill my promise to tell you how I'd made the same journey that you're making. Mine became even more painful, because I'd suffered a broken neck at C-2, the same breaking point as the late Christopher Reeve.

I was more fortunate to only be on the brink of paralysis. At the same time I was recovering from that break, I also was healing from the heartbreak of divorce.

Nobody escapes painful challenges in life and love. How do we find the best path out of pain? Discover how I did this next...

16.

Love Test - What's Good About Floating In Hot Water For A Year?

Pain has been my greatest teacher. Imagine the pain of a broken heart, grieving a divorce, compounded by the pain of a broken neck, disconnecting your brain from controlling your spine.

Imagine pain so pervasive and intense, that it prevented you from resting your head on a pillow, from lifting anything heavier than a feather, from shuffling your feet any faster than a snail's pace.

Imagine your stomach spitting out pain pills on the path through your broken neck, causing so much pain that pills had to be avoided.

Imagine the only relief from pain was found, while doing a back float in a tub of hot water -- during a year or more of recovery.

Now you've imagined the pain I'd experienced after my neck was broken in a fluke injury, which I'd suffered while recovering from the heartbreak of divorce.

Now you may appreciate the lessons pain had taught me, during my year of floating in hot water:

Pain taught me how to love stillness

Outside information felt like a brutal assault that rattled my neck. So I tuned out the media, the telephone and the internet, while I turned my focus inside. If the silences between the notes create beauty and meaning in a song, then silence became the music in my life.

Pain taught me how to rise above it

Every negative thought caused me to sink deeper in pain. So I chose to ignore my inner critic, who'd often complained or focused on negatives. As I let each troubling thought roll off my back, I floated in light-hearted peace.

Pain taught me to feel thankful for each sweet moment of relief

If pain were a monster in a horror film, I shut my eyes and learned to find safety inside-- trusting that all is well, and as it should be in each moment.

Pain taught me to remember the love

Focusing on lost love from my parents who died young, or from my husband who also left me, only caused more pain. As I chose to focus on love that survives physical death or the death of a relationship, I savored all the love that remained in my heart to support me and speed up my recovery.

Pain taught me to express my creativity in ways that lifted my heart, mind and spirit

As I began each 24-hour cycle, I alternated between two hours of floating in hot water to get some sleep, followed by two hours of sitting at my desk to write my first book, which was inspired by my journey from lost love into the fire of love. If a scene or idea didn't lift me up, then I didn't make room for it in my thoughts or in my book.

Pain taught me to ask for help

Facing the threat of paralysis, even if I got bumped gently, I needed help to recover from this serious injury. So I investigated surgical options and weighed the risks of surgery versus nutritional and alternative treatments. Then I chose a safe, non-surgical path toward recovery. It was a great success. Since the experimental, costly treatments were not covered by insurance, I invested most of my savings to recover my best health.

Pain taught me to how to rebuild my body and regain my health

Eating only the best available organic foods, drinking purified water, choosing positive thoughts, actions and supportive friends, and doing some type of exercise each day are proven secrets of real health care reform.

Pain taught me to avoid man-made chemicals, which we naively trust to be safe

As my childhood friends and I ran behind the magical fogging truck that drove through our baseball games on the street every summer, no adult ever tried to stop us. We all were too trusting to even imagine in those days how the DDT sprayed in the fog to kill mosquitoes also could harm our health and even break our bones years after exposure.

Now that we're documenting health threats in thousands of man-made chemicals and in GMO foods, what do we do about it? To recover and protect my health, I avoid all processed and GMO foods, side-effect laden pharmaceuticals and harsh chemicals. I consistently choose safe, wholesome alternatives that cleanse, nourish and rebuild the body without causing any harmful side effects. Thankfully, I feel better than ever.

Pain taught me how to enjoy the exquisite pleasure of self love, inner peace and vibrant health

As I soaked in hot water for over a year, the epsom salts in these baths that detoxed pain and pesticides, also made my hair look like Einstein's and my skin feel like a parched desert. I learned how to transcend physical limitations of my body and let love lift me up as I floated down the glorious river of life -- without getting stuck in the banks of pain.

During my recovery process, which took several years, I wrote a novel inspired by my real-life journey back into health and happiness. My journey became an adventure with help from supportive friends and visionary healers, whom I affectionately call the Tribe Of Blondes. 4/ I named the novel and the Tribe, not for a hair color, but for the resilient, optimistic spirit we need to overcome great challenges and experience great love.

We can't escape life's challenges. We rise up to meet them and even leap over them with resilient, optimistic spirit that unites us in the Tribe Of Light And Love. We are born with this spirit. The secret is to keep it alive. How?

Discover our guiding principles next...

4/ You don't have to face great challenges alone. Find out how I overcame mine with support from the Tribe Of Blondes--resilient optimists who, no matter what life throws you, still believe in great love. I invite you to read the laptop version of my novel as my gift. Gain instant FREE access to Tribe Of Blondes -- the first laptop novel that you read online, which includes an album of songs, videos, and an audiobook of my reading the unabridged novel to you, when you visit www.TribeOfBlondesGiftNovel.com

17.

Shot Down 7 Times/Bounce Back 8 -- Plus 9 Guiding Principles For The Journey From Lost Love To The Fire Of Love

Love Leaves Traces. When you suffer through a lonely bout of lost love, seeing traces of love transforms a painful breakup and rebirth into an adventure in starting fresh and loving again.

Traces of love and wisdom of the ages have inspired the 10 guiding principles that unite men and women in our tribe and fuel our passionate choices and personal triumphs.

10 Principles Guiding Our Journey From Lost Love Into The Fire Of Love:

1. Shot down 7 times, bounce back 8.

When life slams you down, how do you get back up? Developing resilient attitudes and action plans helps you bounce back from any setback. You don't invite anyone to take aim. You do set boundaries to protect your well being. You see life's challenges as chances for personal growth. You celebrate your growth, each time you rise after a fall.

2. Accept finite disappointments, while maintaining infinite optimism.

We are born with an optimistic spirit. The secret is to keep it alive, even while being tested by disappointing losses and challenging circumstances in life and love. We remain optimistic, while facing painful love lessons, by giving silent thanks for our greatest teachers. We're thankful because they presented the challenges that promoted our personal growth. We expect even better times ahead.

3. Feel your pain to fuel your journey into the Fire Of Love.

As mere mortals, we all will face the death of someone we love. We move through each stage of grieving lost love without getting stuck in pain, because we see and celebrate our infinite source of love that remains. We know we are love in our core. We are fueled by the Fire Of Love, which burns away the pain of any loss.

4. Face your fears and move forward anyway.

You won't bury fears or pretend you aren't afraid, because hidden fears surface in hurtful ways. You choose to honor your fears, by accepting them and moving forward anyway.

How? Not by making reckless choices, but by building bridges to stay connected and by knowing that everything is perfect in each moment and as it should be to support your glorious growth.

5. See life's challenges not as a stop sign, but as a yellow light to proceed with care.

In challenging times, you choose your thoughts and actions, your friends and foods that help you feel whole. Affirm out loud each day, "With my thoughts and choices, I create my own happiness, peace, and love."

6. Fall in love with yourself again, using our 5 R's.

* Revive your dreams and take action on them every day.

* Recharge your health, which takes a beating in a bout of lost love, so you look and feel your best.

* Rev up your strengths, so any weaknesses lose power.

* Remain resilient and optimistic, bouncing back from challenges and expecting even better times ahead.

* Remember the love, so your sad, old stories fade away, and you're free to create happy, new ones.

7. Care passionately and be generous with your acts of kindness.

Give plenty of hands-on signs of your tender love to yourself, your family and friends, to our planet and all life on it. Be your own best friend at all times, and treat others with the same loving kindness that promotes even greater love, health and well being.

8. Move from stress and dis-ease to joy, health and love.

Unforgiveness is a source of dis-ease. The antidote: Breathe out un-forgiveness and the pain it causes. Breathe in healing peace and love. Do this exercise several times each day during challenging times. Remind yourself, "This too shall pass, and prepare me." Ask yourself several times each day, "What is the most loving thing I can do for myself right now?" Then do it to feel even more loved and lovable.

9. Turn off bad news media and stay focused on solutions.

What you think about, you bring about. What you see will be, when you take the right actions. When you change the bad news channel and focus on solutions instead of problems, you are more likely to take actions that promote solutions and positive change.

10. Live fully and love deeply, as you savor the joys or challenges in each moment.

You choose to experience maximum joy and love in each moment of your life.

You choose to find love lessons in losses and live happily-ever-after right now, no matter what life throws you, no matter who is or isn't sleeping next to you.

You also choose to be the kind of lover who is happiest, instead of being the kind who feels miserable and confused. How?

Let's find out what kind of lover you are, by taking a simple Love Test next...

18.
Love Test - What Kind Of Lover Is Happiest?

How you love life determines what kind of lover you are. One kind experiences greater happiness than the other. What kind of lover are you?

Find out by taking this simple Love Test:

Do You Ever:

* resist how things are right now?
* complain how things should be?
* place conditions on how people must earn your love?
* decide you'll be happy only under certain circumstances?
* obsess over painful thoughts or feelings?
* carry around sad, old stories?
* feel paralyzed by fear?
* resent happy people or couples in love?

How did you score?

Each YES response reveals where you are a "Lover of How Things Should Be."
This kind of lover often feels miserable and confused about what you need to do to feel more passion and pleasure in life and love.

Each NO response reveals where you are a "Lover of Reality."
This kind of lover accepts circumstances and people however they show up, and understands that you already have everything you need inside you to feel totally loved, lovable, approved of and appreciated.

Are you a "lover of what should be?"

If so, are you willing to change that? You are energized by even greater happiness, when you become a "lover of what is." How?

You turn each YES response into a NO, simply by questioning your thoughts that keep you stuck in pain and disconnected from happiness and love.

The good news is you can do this right now.

All you need to do is ask yourself four simple questions and then turn around the thoughts or fears that torment you, whenever you resist reality.

The process of questioning the mind to find happiness is known as "The Work." This process was developed by Byron Katie. In her book, I Need Your Love - Is That True?, she explains how to stop seeking love, approval and appreciation, and start finding them instead.

Byron Katie has divided "the work" into 5 steps, which you take whenever you want to release a stressful thought or feeling and replace it with a better one. I've summarized how to do "the work" in 5 steps:

1. Write down your most painful thought, feeling, fear or circumstance now or in the past.

It can be a simple statement like, "He/she just walked away, and that means they don't care about me."

Now you question it.

2. Ask yourself, "Is that true?" And, "Can I absolutely know that is true?"

Don't consult the part of you that knows what should be.

The question is -- does this thought match what you know to be true in your deepest sense of reality?

Write down your answers.

3. Explore how you live and react when you believe this thought.

Does it bring you peace or stress?

Does it bring you closer to people you love or separate you?
When you believe this thought, how do you treat yourself and others?

Jot down your answers.

4. Explore who you would be and what life would be like without this thought.

Imagine how it feels to live in the space that opens up when you see your situation or someone's behavior, without that stressful thought.

In our example above, you see someone walk away from you without thinking that they don't care about you.

Jot down how you and your life changes, without that thought.

5. Turn around that tormenting thought, and find three genuine examples of how each turnaround is as true or truer than the original thought.

Consider the reverse or opposite versions of that troubling thought.

In our earlier example of seeing someone walk away and feeling they don't care about you, your turnaround might be:

* I don't care about him/her.
* I don't care about me (whenever I give myself stress and sadness.)
* He/she does care about me.

Now list three genuine examples of how each turnaround is as true or truer than your original statement.

This completes "The Work." I encourage you to write down these four questions and the turnaround step on a notecard. Keep it near you for handy use whenever you have a stressful thought or feeling to reverse, by using the remedy of a hearty dose of reality.

Instead of stressing over a troubling thought, you ask yourself these four questions, embrace the answers and do the turnaround to train yourself to become a lover of what is.

Developing this new Love Habit makes you the kind of lover who experiences the greatest happiness in life and love. Since like attracts like, you attract what you are, not what you want. As a lover of reality, you attract a like-hearted lover with the attitudes and actions that create the happiest life and relationships.

Now, let's explore another kind of relationship that often makes people too uncomfortable to discuss. The breakdown of this relationship is a top cause of breakups and daily stress. Creating a quality relationship in this area is a creative catalyst for a rich life. Let's find out how to revitalize this relationship next...

19.

End Money Worries And Even Double Your Income Doing What You Love

How's your relationship with money? Are you aware that money worries are a common cause of breakups? Money worries also may increase after breaking up a marriage and may send a family into cycles of poverty for generations.

You prevent or reverse that cycle and create a rich relationship with money, by using the remedies you're about to discover.

Find out how to end money worries by achieving your goals without struggle and by doing more of what you love each day in highlights of my radio interview for A Lasting Love with Raymond Aaron.

He is a co-author of the bestselling Chicken Soup for the Parents' Soul, an acclaimed success mentor, and author of Double Your Income Doing What You Love. Raymond gives you a download copy of this book as a gift when you visit www.Aaron.com.

Hadley: Instant Gratification. Some of us think it's a bad thing. But you say, "If it's worth doing, it's worth doing now." So how do we stop delaying gratification and start achieving our best goals right now?

Raymond: If your goal is to end money worries, I teach you how to deposit $1000 to $10,000 in your savings account every month.

If you want to go on more exotic vacations with someone you love, I show you how to take a week's vacation every month, like I do.

As hard as it is for you to believe this, I show you exactly how I do this. And you can, too. It's all in the first chapter of my book, Double Your Income Doing What You Love, which I am giving you for free.

Hadley: I've read your book, and I like using your success tools. Some people may think you use mind games to achieve goals effortlessly.

Yet I know you're showing people how to put the law of attraction into action and tap into universal power that propels you to achieve your goals easily, without struggling. Tell us how that process works.

Raymond: I teach people how to write goals the right way, using my patented process. It's so powerful that the goals seem to achieve themselves so fast, it's like magic. That's why I made up the term, "AutoMagically," to describe it.

Hadley: Some people may not realize there's a right and wrong way to record your goals. You give us step-by-step guidance in your book, which we download at no charge on your website. Getting this success strategy is yet another convincing reason to claim your free book.

Raymond: I still use these strategies every month--not only for financial success, which I have, but also to make sure that my marriage gets better and better every month, which it does.

Hadley: Writing Love Letters is a great way to sustain romance in a relationship. You suggest that we also write Annual Love Letters to ourselves to achieve goals we love. How do we start?

Raymond: You have to write your Annual Love Letters backwards. This is the opposite way of writing a goal, like you want to earn $200,000 a year, when you're currently earning $100,000 a year. That big goal feels heavy and difficult. It makes you afraid you won't achieve it.

Yet if you pretend you're already on the last day of the goal year, looking back at the year and congratulating yourself for achieving this goal, then the bigger your goal, the better.

So I write my annual love letters and one-year goals backwards in the past tense, acting as if I've already achieved them that year. What I say is, "I'm so grateful that I earned $200,000 this year."

Then the law of attraction immediately gets implemented, because your reptilian, subconscious brain doesn't have the ability to discern right from wrong or truth from untruth. That's because when we were cavemen, you didn't have time to determine, "Is this a friend tricking me? Or is this a tiger about to eat me?" You had to react immediately.

So your reptilian, subconscious mind can't tell the difference between that which is real and that which is imaginary.

This means that if you say today, "I'm so grateful I earned $200,000 this year," then your subconscious mind takes that in and starts implementing it.

Hadley: That's true, if you also add this essential step. You must take new actions to get new results you want. This action step was missing in the popular film, "The Secret."

Raymond: I was one of 40 teachers in the world filmed for that movie. One thing I stressed is that you can't just think it and imagine it. You actually have to do something. That could be why I was cut out of that film, which implied you only had to imagine goals to fulfill them.

Hadley: They were selling the fantasy at first. We've just clarified the importance of setting goals and taking new actions to fulfill your goals. This process works with financial or health goals, as well as love goals.

For example, if you want to find love this year, you simply imagine you've already done so. Then every day you give thanks for your great love and great feelings they inspire. Your feelings of love and gratitude attract love, like an irresistible love magnet, and magnetize even more love to you.

I've just thought of another twist on writing goals backwards. Some success coaches recommend that you write your own eulogy when you're young, by listing the top goals you've accomplished during your life, and then living up to them.

Raymond: It's one thing to write your own eulogy, but that's typically too big and too strategic for most people. When you write your goals backwards, one year at a time, then you know exactly what to implement that year.

Hadley: Now that you know how to improve your relationship with money, write annual Love Letters to yourself, achieve your goals "automagically," and do more of what you love each day, you still may be wondering, "When will I be ready to love again, even better than ever?"

Let's find out next...

20.
5 Ways To Love Again, As If It's The First Time

Healing your breakup wounds is the healthy prelude to your romantic recovery. You feel refreshed, renewed and ready to love again, like it's the first time, when you take 5 steps:

1. Erase the battle scars of your breakup or bout of lost love with these exercises:

* Forgive yourself and your former mate for any hurtful actions in the past, by using your favorite forgiveness techniques you've discovered here

* Take good care of your body with therapeutic massage, hot baths, essential oils, manicures and pedicures, which include hand and foot reflexology. Men and women alike experience the revitalizing benefits of these treatments

* Lift your spirits each day with upbeat music, friends, books, time in nature, meditation and daily reflection on beauty and love

* Revive your dreams and take action on them daily, even if only during a coffee break

* Remember the love so your sad, old stories fade away, and you're free to create a happy, new love story

2. Love your body, flaws and all

* Give thanks each day for your personal miracle maker, which heals injuries, fights disease, creates new life and takes you on great adventures in loving and living your dreams

* See any lines as love lines, any sags or extra padding as signs you need a healthy boost of nourishment, movement and self love

* Recharge your health with whole organic foods and safe, holistic healing practices. These include drinking pure water, getting daily exercise, doing deep breathing to feel calm and energized, using guided visualization, meditation, prayer or biofeedback to break through hidden barriers to even greater love, health and happiness you deserve

3. Get your sex muscles in shape

* Do Kegel exercises whenever you're standing in line, sitting at the computer or waiting for a red light to turn green. Women and men do kegels by squeezing the floor of your

pelvis for a few seconds, and then relaxing. Repeat 20 times. Do this exercise a couple times a day to keep your sex muscles strong, so you're ready to enjoy a passionate sex life when you meet your Great Love Match

4. Rev up your sexual desire

* Wake up your libido with natural health care and super foods that support healthy sexual desire. Drink tea made with pure water and cayenne. It's known as the roto-rooter spice, because it keeps blood flowing to sex organs, like those blue pills

* Men and women, who've lost that lovin' feeling, get your hormone levels balanced to optimal levels for healthy desire, as guided by a natural health care practitioner

* Arouse your sexual fantasies with romantic or erotic films and novels about the adventures in finding love and getting the red-hot love life you deserve

* Notice the sexual energy in people you meet, as if you're tuning into their good vibrations and raising your own

5. Get back in the dating world

* Tell your family and friends that you're ready to date, and ask them if they know a good match for you

* Expand your dating horizons beyond your neighborhood or workplace

* Seek out single friends interested in socializing and traveling with you

* Sign up for a lunchtime matchmaking service that introduces singles over lunch

* Join a top online dating site like TribeOfSingles.com Love matches - Love Vacations, which safely introduces you to a community of savvy singles who are seeking their great love match now. Meet in fun video chats, social meetup activities and love vacations to the best spots on earth. Get an exciting love toolkit to choose your great love match and create a great relationship.

* Trust that there is no reason to be alone, at any age, unless you want to be -- since there are millions of singles seeking great love across America and around the world.

5 / I guide your love quest with advice like this and help you chose your great love match in TribeOfSingles.com Love Matches - Love Vacations. To claim your gift membership, sign up at www.TribeOfSingles.com Enter Gift Coupon Code: tribelifetime09. Enjoy your guided love quest as my gift -- ideally until you meet your great love match and get all the love and happiness you deserve.

As you take 5 steps to be ready to love again, even better than ever, notice how you've healed your past and started fresh with a healthy outlook and happy heart.

Give thanks for how you've freed yourself to fall in love again, as if it's the first time. It's as if you've come into existence with all the wisdom and love skills you need to create the life and relationships you love.

Please accept my gifts to guide your ongoing progress next...

21.
Your Gifts and Guides To Even Greater Love and Happiness

Let's celebrate all of the great gifts you are giving yourself, such as deciding to make the brave journey from heartbreak to happiness, and using new love skills to build the new life you love now.

The secret of a successful journey is being totally committed to your forward progress. Remember that your goal is progress, not perfection.

To safeguard your ongoing progress, you may need to set new boundaries, which give limited access into your life to the people who drain your energy, drag you down or derail you from the path you've chosen. This may include limiting your availability to family and friends, who stress you or steal your joy, even if you love them. Why?

People who are negative and unhappy lack the love skills to help you bounce back from setbacks, and feel loved and happy, no matter what life throws you. They may be threatened or jealous of the great strides you are making each day. They may sabotage your progress, because they are afraid you'll leave them behind someday.

You continue to love these people, but not their destructive actions and attitudes. To protect your progress, you become your own best friend. You only invite into your life the people, who support your growth and your vision for the life and relationships you love. You only spend time with people you want to become.

What if you must see negative people at an event with family or friends?

You remain friendly and keep things light. Whenever their critical or defeating behavior begins, you don't engage. You might politely excuse yourself and walk away.

You might say, "When you're finished complaining, let me know. Because I'd like to catch up with your good news."

Doing this encourages people to improve their behavior, if they want to be around you. You also protect your ongoing progress by choosing new friends, who support your growing and becoming the person you want to be.

That's why I formed the Tribe Of Blondes and united positive women and men with the resilient optimistic spirit we need to overcome great challenges and experience the great love and happiness we all deserve.

We're all born with the spirit. The secret is to keep it alive, with help from supportive friends. This spirit is contagious, and you catch it in Tribe of Blondes.

I'd like to give you a gift of Tribe Of Blondes -- my novel inspired by my real-life adventures in starting fresh and finding love after losing a relationship or lover.

You read the laptop version of this novel online, and enjoy its songs, art, videos, plus an audiobook of my reading the unabridged novel to you. Gain instant free access simply by visiting www.TribeOfBlondesGiftNovel.com This is only one of my gifts, which guide you to even greater love and happiness in your new life.

I invite you to download or gain access to all of your gifts by following the instructions in the gift menu below.

And I invite you to keep me posted on your ongoing progress, as you build your best life and get all the love and happiness you deserve.

Hadley Finch

hadley@tribeofsingles.com

YOUR GIFTS FROM HADLEY FINCH

* Gift Laptop Novel with Audiobook by Hadley Finch, reading her unabridged novel:

TRIBE OF BLONDES--Adventures of Breakup Survivors Seeking Love Online And Happiness In Relationships. Enjoy the first laptop novel with songs, art and videos that you view online. It's inspired by Hadley's real-life adventures in starting fresh and finding love online. It includes an audiobook of Hadley reading the unabridged novel to you. Claim instant FREE access to this online novel when you visit: http://www.TribeOfBlondesGiftNovel.com

* Gift Album of Pop Country Love Songs, with lyrics by Hadley Finch:

This upbeat album of songs is called Soulgrass, because it tells a soulful story that adds meat to the bones of its bluegrass, country and pop music mix. The story starts with a breakup, goes through phases of grieving, reviving your dreams and dating again, and it ends up in the Fire Of Love. Isn't that where we all want to be? Hadley shows you how to get there in this album of songs, which are flashbacks to the action in her novel. Download your gift album of songs at http://www.TribeOfBlondesBonusMusic.com

* Gift Access to Archives Of A Lasting Love Radio Show, hosted by Hadley Finch:

Gain instant access to dozens of episodes of A Lasting Love radio show, featuring conversations between Hadley Finch and other top love experts. They share secrets and strategies to find love fast, avoid dating and relationship minefields, pass love tests and move from being alone or being bored to happiness and bliss.

Check out the show **archives of previous episodes** accessed in the menu bar. Download your favorite shows by title/topic, including the episodes which Hadley summarized in 911 Breakup Survival, when you visit http://www.ALastingLove.net

* Gift e-Book by Hadley Finch:

Searching singles avoid dead-end dating and find love fast when you discover 7 new ways to attract great people to date, love and marry in your gift e-book. Gain instant access to your FREE e-book at http://www.IFindLoveFast.com

* Gift of the #1 guided love quest, led by America's Love Guide, Hadley Finch

Once you've made your journey from lost love to the fire of love, you're ready to love again, even better than ever. Hadley Finch guides your love quest and gives you expert dating advice and exciting love toolkit to handle baggage, choose your great love match and create a blissfully happy, passionate relationship in TribeOfSingles.com Love Matches-Love Vacations where great singles find a great love match.

Meet our community of positive, accomplished men and women on your love wavelength (seeking their great love match now) during fun video chats, in live meetup events and in love vacations to the best spots on earth.

Remember the great love you are seeking is seeking you. Give your great love the chance to find you in our dating site for resilient optimists who, no matter what life throws you, still believe in great love. You find great love and great love skills to build your dream life and relationship during a guided love quest in TribeOfSingles.com

To claim your gift membership, sign up at https://www.TribeOfSingles.com

As you subscribe, enter Gift Coupon Code: tribelifetime09

Enjoy your FREE Guided Love Quest, ideally until you meet your great love match and get the red-hot love life you deserve.

MY NOTES:

MY NOTES:

www.ingramcontent.com/pod-product-compliance
Lightning Source LLC
La Vergne TN
LVHW051158080426
835508LV00021B/2682